Self-Acceptance Journal

This Journal belongs to:

————————————————
NAME

I am free to accept myself as I am.

Introduction

Welcome! This is your own personal Self-Acceptance Journal. What does that mean? It means you have an opportunity to discover how wonderful you are just as you are.

This journal gives all your self-doubts, fears, concerns, and worries a place to go. By journaling and working through these negative thoughts and emotions, you will be giving yourself permission to be free... free from thinking you are not enough... free to be who you are, as you are!

During these turbulent times in your life when your body is changing physically and your emotions are sweeping you off your feet, it is hard to remember that you are OK just as you are. You may feel alone at times. You may feel nobody understands. You may also feel that life seems really hard and that you can't get anything "right."

I can tell you that you are not alone, you are understood, and you are very loved.
You are perfect as you are.

As you step into the truth of loving yourself just as you are, you will more easily love and appreciate others too. You will be able to relax and "go with the flow".

It isn't always easy to ride the waves of life. My hope is that this self-acceptance journal will be a surfboard of sorts... helping you learn to surf these waves.

I encourage you to return to this journal again and

again as needed. It will offer you a safe harbor to process all that is going on in your life. It will give you a place to reflect and see how you have grown. Our life waves never stop but we do learn to surf better and better.

May you enjoy the unfolding process of stepping into the goodness and beauty of who you already are! You matter!

Much Love!

Dory Jolin

www.doryjolin.com

What To Expect

This journal is a tool to help you on your self-acceptance path. It is divided into sections that will ask you to write or draw about a self-acceptance topic as it pertains to you. The following are the individual sections of the journal.

This section is about getting those things you do not like about yourself down on paper. These are your "rocks". (The term "rocks" is described in more detail in this section).

This section will give you a place to discover where your rocks originated and how they were formed.

After you discover where your rocks came from, you will let them go and step into self-acceptance.

This section gives you the space to celebrate who you are right now. This is where you can write down what you like about yourself.

Your rocks will continue to roll into your light bowl. They may come in smaller or less frequently, but they still roll in. This is where you can quickly release those new rocks.

At the end of the journal you will have plenty of space to keep a gratitude list. Appreciation helps us accept ourselves and those around us. Gratitude is a quick and easy way to keep your inner light bowl shining.

Take your time in each section. It is not a race. As with most things in life, the more you put into it, the more you will get out of it.

To start with, you may find it easiest to work in the order the sections are laid out. The more you work with it, the more you may find yourself led to spend time in one section or another, without regards to a specific order. Know that there is no right or wrong way to use this journal. Trust your instincts.

Self-Acceptance healing is an ongoing journey. It takes time and as you grow you may repeat these steps as often as you need. This journal is like a tool in your toolbox helping you move through all that life has to offer and giving you the power to love yourself as you are!

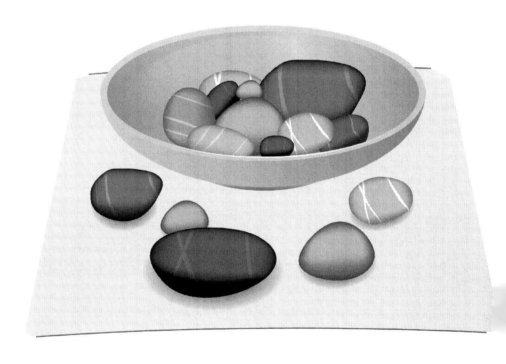

Your "Rocks"

There is a Hawaiian spiritual tradition that believes when a child is born, he/she is like a bowl of light, shining bright and clear. As the child grows the bowls start to fill with rocks. These rocks are fears, insecurities, self-doubts, or past pains that have not been healed. They are thoughts like "you are not good enough", "you are not smart", or "you do everything wrong."

These rocks are created over time and sometimes they come from adults, teachers, or friends who have passed on some of their own rocks to you. These rocks are not the truth of who you are.

Let's make a rock garden now. List all the things that you feel are not right about yourself. Be honest about your feelings. Take your time. Make lists. Draw pictures. Get creative!

I am radiant.

I have permission to be who I am.

I am a perfect expression of love.

I forgive myself.

I am doing the best I can.

I see the colors of the rainbow enfolding me now.

My heart is open and I am safe.

I am in charge of my thoughts.
I choose the good ones.

I think happy thoughts and my heart feels good.

Tears are essential for clearing past pain.

I allow myself to cry. It helps me heal.

I am safe to be myself.

I let go of what I cannot control.

Letting go helps me feel peaceful.

Learning About Your "Rocks"

Now that you have identified your rocks, let's take some time to help you learn how these rocks formed.

Pick the first rock you would like to remove. What is it? Where did it come from? Do you remember when it started to form over your light? If you don't remember that is OK. Just give it a try. Write about how this rock came to be.

For example, I had a thought that I never looked right. I was never skinny enough, pretty enough, and never had the right clothes to wear. When I looked into these thoughts I discovered I had learned these messages from my grandmother and mother. I needed to work out my feelings concerning these old messages, accept where they came from, accept me just how I am... and then I was able to forgive. This is just one example. Give it a try yourself and see if you can discover where your rocks formed.

I matter!

I am loved.

I am free to be me!

I am perfect as I am.

I forgive myself and others.

I care deeply about myself.

I forgive easily.

I am willing to let go.

I am amazing just the way I am.

It is OK to ask for help.

I am at peace with myself.

I am beautiful just as I am.

Wisdom and truth are my guides.

I don't always have to understand or figure things out.

Dealing With Your "Rocks"

Here is a little meditation for you to use to help you step into self-acceptance.

> *(Breathe in, breathe out. Breathe in, breathe out.)*
> *Just for right now accept yourself just as you are in*
> *this very moment. Let go of the thoughts that you*
> *need to be like someone else or that you could do*
> *better in some area of your life.*
>
> *Accept that where you are right now is good*
> *enough. The past is done. The future is not here*
> *yet. You are right here in this moment.*
>
> *Just for right now accept that you are enough.*
> *You are perfect as you are. Let go...breathe in the*
> *acceptance that surrounds you.*

You may step into self-acceptance any time you'd like. Know that "all that has been" and "all that will be" is not in this very moment and has no real power over you. As you move through acceptance of yourself you will be able to forgive and you will be able to let the rocks roll away. You will begin to uncover your beautiful, bright inner light that allows you to be yourself.

Take some time and look at your rocks again. Painful rocks need attention. When you look at your rocks, what do they say? Do you want to keep them? Can you put them in a different spot? Do you want to gently move them off your inner bowl of light? Are you ready to have God take them for you? Do you want to turn them into light by forgiving them and placing them in your heart?

Surround your rocks with love. They can be sent away or loved into light. The choice is yours.

I speak loving words to myself.

I am happy to be me!

I listen with my heart.

I like who I am becoming.

I am thankful.

I give myself permission to let go and enjoy life.

The past is over; the future awaits;
now is all that matters.

I am a blessing to everyone in my life, including myself.

I am becoming my own best friend.

I am learning all the time.

Self-love is an inside job.

Who I am is enough.

I am a student and a teacher.

Being different is a gift.

Celebrating You

You have just completed dealing with your rocks. Great Job! Now you are ready for another important step on your self-acceptance journey.

On the following pages, make a list of all the things you like about yourself. Draw pictures. Create what you love about yourself any way you feel guided.

If you have a hard time getting started in this section, here's a hint to get you going. You've just completed the "Dealing With Your Rocks" section of this journal. You have done the work to clear out your light bowl. That is a major accomplishment, taking an enormous amount of courage! That is DEFINITELY something to celebrate.

I celebrate the person I am today!

I am enough!

There is not another person
just like me in the whole world!

I am a perfect expression of God's love.

I enjoy being alive.

I am free to express myself.

I love my life.

I am grateful for my family and friends.

I am a gift in this world.

I am likable.

I love myself as I am.

I am awesome.

My inner light shines bright and shows me the way.

I am joy.

Caring For Your Daily "Rocks"

Each day you experience new people, new situations, and new thoughts. So while you may feel free of those pesky rocks for a while, new ones are constantly rolling in.

The good news is that you will get better at recognizing these rocks as they appear. This awareness allows you to deal with the rocks effectively, before they weigh you down. When a new rock appears in your bowl, the temptation is to immediately try to let it go. I encourage you to take some time with your rocks. Does it look like any of your other rocks? Is there a past experience attached to it? Write it down. Draw it.

I encourage you to talk about those rocks that continually resurface. Discuss them with a parent, caregiver or safe adult. See what that trusted individual may have to say about letting go of these particular rocks.

I am courageous.

I let go with ease.

I am smart.

I give myself permission to be who I am.

I know when to ask for help.

I am not alone.

I use kind words when talking to myself and others.

Today is what matters most.

I allow myself to feel calm.

I am in control.

Today I will be myself.

My life is good.

I know what's best for me.

Kindness is my superpower.

Gratitude

You have done an amazing job for yourself. If you feel like you have some rocks that just won't budge, ask for help. You matter! You are perfect as you are!

On the following pages you may write all that you are grateful for... all that you appreciate about your life.

I rock!

I am grateful!

Today is the start of a new beginning.

I love my world.

I am happy to be alive.

Blessings are manifesting all around me.

I am a miracle.

Today I am listening to my inner wisdom.

I have a lot of goodness to share.

I listen and trust.

I have faith.

Thank you!

I am a blessing.

I hear the truth which is always love.

I am perfectly imperfect as I am.

A Message From Dory

I have been using self-acceptance healing for a big part of my life. I know sometimes it can get tricky. If you feel you may need a little extra help, please let your parent or caregiver know. You may also contact me if your parent or caregiver says it is OK. I help preteenagers and teenagers at my healing center and over the phone.

May you love and accept yourself just as you are!

You Matter!

Blessings

Dory

Made in the USA
Middletown, DE
23 May 2016